Useful Insights and Ideas to Help Parents Connect Emotionally

Joyous Child Joyous Parent is a swift antidote to decaying family relationships. Easy to read and implement, Connie's book can help you and your children grow happily together.
—Pat Farenga, author *Teach Your Own: The John Holt Book of Homeschooling*

Joyous Child, Joyous Parent is chock full of wonderful ideas and suggestions for parents who recognize the importance of connecting with their children and want to reap the rewards of a rich parenting experience that enhances their lives and the lives of their children. —Marilyn Milos, Founder and Executive Director, National Organization of Circumcision Information Resource Centers (NOCIRC)

A few minutes each day is all it takes to set the stage to a more joyous and fulfilling connection with your child—and your world. For this is not just about loving your child, it's also about loving yourself and your world. Whether you pause to reflect on just one of these pages for a few minutes daily, weekly, whenever—your relationship with your child and your life will be all the more joyful and fulfilling for it.
—Meryn Callander, President and Cofounder, Alliance for Transforming the Lives of Children (aTLC)

Anyone who interacts with children in any way can dabble in this book for general inspiration. You can open any page and read something that is intriguing, something you even know about but have perhaps forgotten. The ten top tips are so important it is amazing that they can be laid out so simply. —Helen Hughes, Founder of Windsor House, a democratic, parent-participation public school

Give the gift of joy to yourself and your child.

See what others are saying about Connie's Joy with Children programs:

I like your balanced approach. Both parents and children win! —Mary Carp, Los Altos, CA

I learned how to be the person my child wants to have as his father. —Peter Lipscomb, Santa Fe, NM

Thank you, as always, for your helpful words in your wonderful newsletter and book. Your words are like balm to the struggling perfectionist in me. —Sara Richey, San Jose, CA

The Parenting with Joy Training was a lifesaver for our family. We saw changes immediately. Using the principles and exercises from the class, I learned to listen to my son more and struggle with him less. My husband and I are much more on the same page with our parenting. Our relationship is better because of it. —Isabel Parlett, Santa Fe, NM

I now feel my son is a fun person to be around—even for all day! —Sharon Johnson, Cotati, CA

Joyous Child, Joyous Parent

60 Ways to Have More Fun and Joy with Your Child

Connie Allen, M.A.

Metacreative Press
True Wisdom Series

Information provided in this book is intended for educational and support purposes only and must not be considered to be a substitute for therapy provided by your own mental health professional.

Allen, Connie.
Joyous Child, Joyous Parent: 60 Ways to Have More Fun and Joy with Your Child

ISBN 978-0-9796669-0-2

First Edition

1 0   9   8   7   6   5   4   3   2   1

This book is lovingly dedicated to all the young people who have trusted and guided me along the way.

Contents

Welcome

Preface

All children are naturally creative, capable, loving people who want to succeed in life and to have a joyous, loving connection with you. Your role is to support them in trusting themselves so they can express their natural gifts and be the amazing people they naturally are.

When I talk with parents, I find they experience more of the struggle and worry of parenting and less of the joy and fun they desire. They feel unsure how to handle situations with their child. They want to do the right thing and are unclear what that is. They yell and feel frustrated more than they feel they should.

If you're like most parents, you feel caught between being too permissive and too authoritarian with your child. You feel unclear when to draw the line and set a limit and when to say "Yes" and nurture your child's wonderful spirit. You know both are important to your child's emotional and social development; but you feel confused about what is the right thing to do.

The key to having the joy and connection with your child that you desire is to realize there is only one person whose behavior you can change. It is your own. Do not try to change your child. Instead learn how you can improve your own behavior, and your child's behavior will improve in response to the positive, empowering changes you make.

This book is designed to help you to discover new understandings of your child and what he needs from you. Transforming or expanding your perception is one of the most powerful and effective ways you can change and grow as a person and a parent. Your perception is your interpretation of a behavior or situation. It is the meaning you place on what is happening. When you master the art of shifting to more positive perceptions, you and your child will be happier.

You can always improve your relationships with children. This book contains ideas to help you have more joy and connection with the children in your life whether they are 2, 15, or 50 years old.

As a mother, teacher, coach, and trainer, I developed this powerful perspective over 30 years of relating with children of all ages and from diverse backgrounds. I invite you to try these ideas and be inspired by what is possible.

I wish you a joyous journey connecting with the children you love!

Connie

Connie Allen, MA
Family and Education Coach
Joy With Children
Connie@JoyWithChildren.com
http://JoyWithChildren.com

Joyous Child, Joyous Parent

Your children are not your children.

They are the sons and daughters of Life's longing for itself.

They come through you but not from you,

And though they are with you yet they belong not to you.

YOU may give them your love but not your thoughts,

For they have their own thoughts.

You may house their bodies but not their souls,

For their souls dwell in the house of to-morrow, which you cannot visit, not even in your dreams.

You may strive to be like them, but seek not to make them like you.

For life goes not backward nor tarries with yesterday.

You are the bows from which your children as living arrows are sent forth.

The archer sees the mark upon the path of the infinite, and He bends you with His might that His arrows may go swift and far.

Let your bending in the Archer's hand be for gladness;

For even as He loves the arrow that flies, so He loves also the bow that is stable.

Kahlil Gibran, The Prophet

Have a More Joyous Relationship with Your Child

Even though you and your child love each other, if you're like most parents, you experience repetitive difficult situations with your child. You may have frustrating interactions with one another, or you may feel the sadness of watching your child struggle with a personal challenge. Left to continue, these difficulties negatively affect you and your child and tend to increase over time.

Take action now. You have in your hands a powerful tool to find effective solutions to your challenging concerns. Use this book to get the results you want.

If you find yourself feeling guilty and being hard on yourself for things you wish you were doing differently, please love and be compassionate toward yourself. When you are self-critical, both you and your child suffer.

Instead find ways to acknowledge yourself for all you do well. You already have many excellent parenting skills and you have the ability to be an even better parent. Recognize and appreciate your desire and commitment to be the best parent you can be. This is a powerful foundation upon which you can build.

Reading the entire book at one time may be overwhelming; so choose the section that seems most relevant at the moment. Read it carefully to understand the concepts and how they relate to you and your child.

The learning from this book does not end after you've read it once. Read it again and again to further develop your skills to build a close connection with your child. When you have a difficult time knowing how to handle a situation, open the book at random and see what jumps out at you. It might be the perfect answer to your dilemma.

Have a More Joyous Relationship with Your Child

To discover new possibilities of authentic trust and connection with your child, here are some steps you can follow.

- ★ **Review** all 60 ideas to find which ones are most appropriate to your situation and the areas in which you want to grow.

- ★ **Select** 5 to 10 ideas you want to work on, and put a star beside them.

- ★ **Decide** which idea is most important, and find at least one specific action you can take to implement this idea.

- ★ **Put** today's date beside it and follow through on your action for at least one week.

- ★ **Choose** the next important idea and continue the process.

By using this approach, the idea and your ability to use it effectively integrate more deeply into your psyche; it becomes easier to make better choices.

My use of the term "your child" in this book is for ease of communication only. It is not meant to imply ownership or parenthood, but simply refers to the child with whom you relate. When you read the ideas, please substitute in your mind the relationship you have with a child, whether it's your grandchild, your student, your niece, or a friend's child.

I have found the terminology "he or she" or "he/she" to be awkward. To avoid gender bias, I have alternated the use of masculine and feminine pronouns throughout.

You may notice an overlap of ideas among the sections. This occurs because relationships are holistic and holographic, not linear. The interconnected ideas in this book weave together to empower and nurture your relationship with your child.

Raising a happy, successful child is a continuous process of discovery. As your child grows and changes, the core strategies in this book stay the same. The implementation changes to suit your child's level of development and uniqueness.

Top Ten Tips

These top 10 tips are powerful even though they may appear to be obvious and simple. If you focus on doing these 10 tips well, you and your child will flourish as the unique individuals you are. Your relationship with your child will become more magnificent and joyous.

– 1 –

Say "Yes!" to your child in as many ways as you can.

Children need abundant opportunities to express and be themselves. When they are encouraged and allowed to find their own answers, they become wise choice makers who more fully enjoy their lives. Frequent rules—no's, should's, and have-to's—break your child's spirit. He loses his connection to his inner knowing and sense of self.

- 2 -

Be clear when you need to set a limit with your child.

Only set a boundary when it is very important to you. Then mean what you say. When you have too many rules and rules that change, your child may feel confused, insecure, frustrated, angry or overwhelmed. Threats, bribes, criticism, and lectures have little positive, long-term impact and may actually have a negative outcome.

- 3 -

Ensure both you and your child feel happy and nurtured by your relationship.

You can't make your child feel happy, but you can create an emotionally healthy environment for her that makes it easy for her to choose and create her own happiness. If either of you feel discontented with any aspect of your relationship, then together find a way to have your relationship be mutually fulfilling and nurturing.

– 4 –

Play with him.

It's good for both of you. Play is essential to your child's emotional, social, intellectual, and physical development. He learns from exploring and experiencing the world in his unique way. When you play with your child, you develop a closer emotional connection and understand him more deeply. Plus, you become more relaxed and light-hearted.

− 5 −

Go on fun adventures together!

Do something new that allows you both to experience new realities and perspectives. Having new experiences gives your child greater self-confidence and a broader awareness of herself in the world. She develops skills for handling new situations in life.

– 6 –

Be authentically yourself.

This is essential and so often missed. Your child needs to know you as the person you are. No one is perfect no matter how hard they try. Responsibly and honestly tell your child how you feel. It confuses his sense of reality when you pretend to feel or be something you are not. In fact, trying to be the perfect parent gets in the way of your loving connection with your child.

- 7 -

Become more fully yourself.

Most of us choose to live within a narrow framework when innumerable options are available to us. Be willing to expand your perspective of yourself, of children, and of life. As you become more aware and more fully yourself, you create a more loving and fun relationship with your child.

– 8 –

Listen to your child.

She needs it, and you will learn much. We often believe we're listening to children, when we're really trying to get them to listen to us. Instead, listen with a sincere desire to hear her perspective and to have more understanding.

- 9 -

Open your heart to loving him.

You can never love your child too much. Breathe into your heart and expand your capacity to love and be loved. Open yourself to the preciousness of a close emotional connection with your child.

– 10 –

Enjoy her as fully as you can every moment.

Life and time do not stand still. No matter how many times you hear it, you don't fully understand it until she's grown and walking out the door. Children grow up and become adults whether you enjoy and love them or not.

Joyous Child, Joyous Parent

It is only with the heart that one can see rightly.
What is essential is invisible to the eye.

Antoine de Saint-Exupery
The Little Prince

Nurture Your Child

Love

– 11 –

Focus on your heart-felt love for your child.

Let it guide you in making choices. In most situations, your loving heart knows what's best.

- 12 -

Expect wonderfulness from your child most of the time.

Every child has an inner core of good-heartedness and a desire to connect. When you recognize and acknowledge his innate beingness, you nurture his emotional wholeness. Look for it. If your child is struggling in any way, seek guidance from someone you trust.

– 13 –

Let yourself be loved by your child.

A child's love has an open innocence that is a joy to receive. Treasure it as the precious gift it is.

Joyous Child, Joyous Parent

Enjoy

– 14 –

**Spend quality time with your child
every day.**

This helps you know each other and keeps you close. Few things are more important to you and to society than the time you spend with your child, even if you're sharing the routine tasks of life.

– 15 –

Spend time in nature with your child.

Take a hike or go to the beach, whatever is near you. This is a time to persevere even if your child complains of being bored. It will grow on her (and you) and will be a source of peace and inspiration for her throughout her life.

– 16 –

Create regular, fun times together.

Make these times one of your highest priorities and schedule them in your weekly plans. These times solidify your relationship and provide some of your fondest memories.

Joyous Child, Joyous Parent

Accept

– 17 –

Value your child as a unique, whole person whose thoughts, feelings, and desires are separate from yours.

You can never make him be the person you want him to be, nor is it a good idea to try.

- 18 -

Accept your child's choices as much as possible about things that directly affect her.

This helps her be a wise choice-maker now and in the future. It also dramatically reduces power struggles between the two of you.

Appreciate

– 19 –

Be aware of the big things and small things your child does to cooperate and to please you.

It's easy to overlook these behaviors or to take them for granted. When you focus on these cooperative behaviors, you perceive your child more clearly. It also builds his self-confidence.

– 20 –

Look for your child's strengths and positive qualities.

This is especially important if you or your child have stopped being able to see them.

- 21 -

**Tell your child what you honestly
enjoy and admire about her.**

This includes natural and learned abilities,
personal qualities, and her skill in performing a
specific task. It will bring joy to your child's heart
and will help her have a realistic appreciation of her
skills and talents.

Joyous Child, Joyous Parent

Observe

– 22 –

Observe your child's responses to your actions and to situations.

What do they tell you? You will learn much about your child's needs, capabilities, challenges, and emotional well-being through these observations.

- 23 -

Look for the reasons your child habitually doesn't listen or do what you ask.

There is always an important reason for this kind of behavior. Children only do so-called "bad" things for what they perceive to be good reasons.

- 24 -

Be aware of negative, unhappy, uncooperative patterns of behavior in your child and in yourself.

These are warnings that something does not feel good to you or your child. Action needs to be taken. Seek guidance from someone who deeply understands you and your child.

Joyous Child, Joyous Parent

Listen

- 25 -

**Listen intently, sincerely, and with an
open heart to what your child says.**

This is necessary at all ages and lays the
foundation for honest, open communication. This
becomes increasingly important as your child
matures and the topics of discussion become more
life-altering.

– 26 –

Consider thoughtfully what your child tells you.

Children speak from their emotions and mean what they're saying—at the moment. You gain important insights about your child by listening and perceiving situations through his eyes.

Speak

- 27 -

**Talk with your child in a calm,
respectful voice as much as possible.**

This can be challenging when you feel
emotionally upset, but it is especially important at
these times.

- 28 -

**Express how you honestly feel and
what you want in a given situation,
not how you believe a "good person"
or a "good parent" should feel.**

This increases trust and understanding between you. There are no right or wrong feelings you or your child can have.

- 29 -

Ask questions with a sincere desire to hear an honest, unexpected answer.

Children recognize questions with "right" and "wrong" answers embedded in them. Your child will often give you the answer she believes you want to hear, even if it is not her truth.

– 30 –

Ask one specific question at a time.

This improves your communication and connection. A flurry of emotional questions and statements overwhelms your child and makes it hard for him to understand or respond to what you are saying.

- 31 -

Respond to what she did,
not why she did it.

No one truly knows why she does anything. Everyone, including your child, makes choices based on what feels right at the moment. Asking "why" is a detour that takes you nowhere.

Joyous Child, Joyous Parent

Trust

- 32 -

**Trust your child to know what is best
for him and to make his own choices.**

This is one of the most difficult aspects of relating
with your child—recognizing and allowing your child's
natural ability to make wise choices and to learn from
his mistakes. As he develops his choice-making skills,
his self-confidence increases and he becomes more
skilled in knowing what is best for him.

- 33 -

Limit the times you tell your child what to do.

Children need to be allowed to think for themselves. This helps them to be independent, confident, and self-reliant both now and in the future.

– 34 –

Trust your child's natural timetable of growth and development.

As difficult as it may be to believe, your child knows what she's ready for next. She knows when she is ready to go down the slide unassisted, even when she sometimes hurts herself. When you try to make your child conform to society's or your developmental expectations, you limit her emotional wholeness and sense of self.

- 35 -

Let your child make decisions for himself.

This includes the way he decorates his room, the grades he wants in school, the words he wants to say to others. The process of life gives him continuous feedback from which he learns how to make improved choices about taking good care of himself.

Trust

To trust children we must first learn to trust ourselves...and most of us were taught as children that we could not be trusted.

John Holt

Joyous Child, Joyous Parent

Guide

– 36 –

**Let your child follow her own
interests, which may not be yours.**

Every activity or project she chooses contributes
to her future development and her knowledge of
herself and life. She will introduce you to new
interests or experiences you can share together.

– 37 –

Discover and encourage your child's strengths, talents, and interests.

Every child has special gifts. Your genuine encouragement, interest, and enthusiasm help him develop his unique positive abilities and to risk trying something new.

- 38 -

Introduce your child to a variety of experiences, including books, theater, sports events, and museums.

These opportunities give your child a broader range of life-experience from which to make choices about her own interests. They spark her curiosity and add to her knowledge base. The broader her knowledge base, the easier she is able to learn and integrate new ideas and concepts.

- 39 -

Include your child in your projects at home and away from home as much as possible.

Let him help you. He enjoys learning "big people" skills and sharing new experiences with you. It makes him more capable, confident, and competent in all areas of his life. It also brings you closer together.

– 40 –

Eliminate your use of threats to control or manipulate your child.

Threats are meant to frighten a child—not the kind of feeling you want your child to associate with you. Threats insult a child's integrity, no matter how you do it and no matter what the results in the moment. Using threats with your child can sometimes be effective in the moment, but you and your child pay a huge price over time.

– 41 –

Learn to motivate your child without the use of bribes or rewards.

The use of rewards quickly becomes a never-ending pattern in which your child asks, "What do I get if I do it?" Your child will naturally and easily do positive things that please you when she is happy and has a good relationship with herself and with you.

Nurture
Yourself

Take Care of Yourself

Taking care of yourself is essential to raise happy, successful children. A relationship involves two people. It is necessary that both people — you and your child — feel satisfied with the relationship if it is to be rewarding to either one of you.

– 42 –

Make taking care of yourself a high priority.

When you choose to compromise yourself for your child's welfare, over time you feel frustrated and powerless. When you neglect your own well-being, you hurt your child and your relationship as well. By observing you, your child develops his own skills to positively take good care of himself.

– 43 –

Appreciate the good things in your life.

It's a common human pattern to focus on problems and difficulties and to take for granted the blessings you have, including your child and others you love. Gratitude for what you have brightens your day as well as those around you.

– 44 –

Make choices based on your priorities.

Clarity is essential in our fast-paced modern times. When you choose to follow your priorities, you'll spend more time with your child and have more fun. An emotionally-nurturing relationship with your child brings you both the joy, love, and harmony you seek.

- 45 -

Be aware of your feelings and emotional reactions.

As a culture, we pay more attention to our actions and thoughts than we do to our emotions. Yet your emotions affect your behavior, words, tone of voice, and your response to your child. They powerfully impact your relationship with your child and how she perceives you.

– 46 –

Participate in activities you enjoy, even if it means having less time with your child.

These activities keep you vital, alive, and happy for the time you have with your child. They are a necessary component of having quality time together. Children learn how to live fully by watching you.

- 47 -

Slow down your pace of living if you are constantly rushing.

This is one of the biggest challenges parents face. To have a close connection with anyone, you must be present in the moment. A slower pace makes you more aware of your own needs and feelings as well as those of your child.

- 48 -

Learn to say "No" to the requests and needs of others, including family, friends, and groups of which you are a member.

Your enjoyment of life needs to be your highest priority. Giving your time, energy and attention to meet someone else's needs or to solve their problem can diminish your own quality of life. When you say "Yes" to help someone, make sure it is fulfilling to you and gives you pleasure.

- 49 -

Simplify. Simplify. Simplify.

Your child cares about you and a close connection with you more than material possessions. One of the ways you teach materialism is through your choices. Find ways to eliminate or reduce your non-essential tasks and possessions that don't reflect your true priorities.

- 50 -

Take good care of the physical needs of your body.

Engage in fun physical activities by yourself and with others, eat healthy food, get the sleep your body wants, and avoid things you know are harmful to your body. Feeling good physically gives you energy to create a positive life for you and your child. It also models the values you want to teach.

– 51 –

Spend time frequently in nature.

Nurture yourself with quiet time and walks to help you reconnect with yourself, to clarify your priorities, and to let new ideas rise to the surface of your awareness. Nature is a powerful ally throughout your life, including times of stress. Nature helps you be present in the precious moments of life and with your child.

- 52 -

Make time daily for quiet, centered reflection.

This practice helps you relax, listen to yourself more deeply, and be more insightful regarding challenging situations. It deepens your understanding and awareness of yourself and others. The improved quality of life you gain more than makes up for the time you spend.

Agree

Win-win agreements are a powerful tool to create ease and harmony in your relationship with your child. They are essential for mutual joy and self-empowerment.

– 53 –

Schedule time when you and your child are relaxed to work out solutions to your repetitive, difficult interactions.

When you try to resolve them in the heat of the moment, it's hard to step out of the behavior pattern you have created together. Repeating destructive patterns of conflict and disagreement only serve to create more distance between you.

– 54 –

**Perceive your child as a partner who
wants to easily get along with you.**

When you see your child as out to get you in any
way, you dramatically reduce the possibilities
available to both of you. Inability to create a
harmonious, cooperative partnership with your child
limits you and your child's emotional wholeness and
the trust you feel toward one another.

- 55 -

Create win-win agreements with your child in which you and your child both feel good about the outcome.

When you each have what matters most to you, you both feel empowered and nurtured by your relationship. You work as allies to have what you both want. Your child flourishes and so do you.

Set Limits

Most likely, you make too many rules—about things that don't directly affect you, about things your child needs to decide for himself, about inconsequential things—that you are then unable to consistently follow-through on. Your child feels confused and frustrated because he has little power to make choices, and the rules are unclear and too numerous to remember.

Instead of establishing rules for your child, set your limits. Rules are regulations designed to control your child's behavior and to make him conform. They are should's. Limits are the furthest boundary to which your child's behavior can extend. Limits give your child more freedom to express herself, up to your limit.

The goal of setting limits is never punishment. Punishment is intended to make a child feel hurt, pain, shame, fear, or guilt—not the kind of feelings you want your child to associate with you. Punishment seldom prevents the behavior from recurring, and it damages your child's self-confidence and your relationship with your child.

The primary purpose of setting limits with children is to take care of yourself by making your life easier and more enjoyable for you. It is not to teach your child self-control, responsibility or how to "behave right." Your child will develop these skills in response to your actions and her life experiences.

- 56 -

Establish a few clear guidelines of what you need for yourself in relationship with your child.

This requires self-exploration — your feelings, values, priorities, what you enjoy and don't enjoy about your interactions with your child. This clarity creates a close emotional connection and feelings of safety for your child.

– 57 –

Tell your child what you want.

You are more effective when you tell him what you want instead of what you don't want. The negative only draws attention to what you don't want and provides no clarity about what you do want.

− 58 −

Speak in a voice that is calm, certain, and respectful.

When you talk with your child in an angry, accusing, or pleading manner, you make it more difficult for your child to follow through on what you are saying. She will hear and react to your tone of voice rather than to your words.

– 59 –

Remember it is okay to set limits with your child and to mean it.

Your child needs capable, clear, compassionate adults who follow through on the boundaries they set. This helps him feel loved and safe. You are the "ground" on which your child builds his life. Make it solid ground.

– 60 –

Set clear boundaries with your child, and be prepared to follow through with your action.

Explanations and frequent verbal reminders seldom alter your child's choices. They deplete your energy and diminish your emotional connection with your child.

Have More Fun and Joy as a Parent!

If you enjoyed the information and ideas in this book, you will want to learn more and integrate this approach to parenting more deeply into your life. This book is just the beginning. Changing your behavior requires frequent reminders over time and support to keep on track. It is easy to get caught up in the busyness of life and to go back to the old ways of interacting with your child.

Here are trainings and resources we offer to expand your ability to empower your child's emotional and spiritual wholeness.

Subscribe to My Newsletter

Subscribe to *Joy with Children*, a free online newsletter for people who want to nurture their child's emotional wholeness.

You may think you know and understand your child well, but what I've found is that parents often find it hard to see through their child's eyes. In our culture, we aren't trained to pay attention to or to understand emotions very well. Children often experience loneliness, self-doubt and sadness of which their parents are unaware.

When you subscribe to *Joy with Children*, you'll receive my free twice-monthly newsletter filled with tips, practical suggestions, and essential insights. You'll also receive a free information-packed guide and the latest information about my upcoming workshops, trainings, and free teleclasses.

Joy with Children will help you have more of the ease and joy of parenting and less of the stress and struggle. To subscribe, simply complete the short form on my web site at http://www.joywithchildren.com.

Register for the Parenting with Joy Training

Parenting can be a deeply joyous, fulfilling experience. It can also be challenging, frustrating, and painful when your interactions with your child are difficult or you see your child struggling. You may wonder if you're doing everything you can to be the parent you most want to be.

Parents love their kids, but they get into trouble because the tools they have often focus on behavior and not emotional wholeness. Emotional wholeness is a state of being who you are that gives you and your child a strong sense of personal identity and confidence.

You may believe that your child is doing well because he is mostly well-behaved, but what I've discovered is that often parents do not realize how their child is feeling emotionally. When you learn how to observe the signs of how your child is doing emotionally, you become powerfully effective in nurturing his emotional wholeness.

People lament that children do not come with a manual, but what I've found is that every child comes with his own manual. The Parenting with Joy Training teaches you how to read this manual and how to respond in ways that nurture your child's emotional and spiritual wholeness. When your child feels deeply nurtured in being who she is, she becomes happier and more cooperative, confident, and loving.

In the Parenting with Joy Training, you learn the six essential ingredients to having a joyous, loving relationship with your child. Plus you discover and develop effective parenting skills, such as setting limits and creating win-win agreements, which dramatically reduce your stress and makes parenting so much more fun.

Every idea in this book guides you to make dramatic improvements in your relationship with your child. If you want more help applying them in real life with your unique child and situation, the Parenting with Joy Training is perfect. You will be delighted with the discoveries you make and the wonderful changes you see happen. To learn more, visit the following web page: http://www.joywithchildren.com.

Schedule a Coaching Session

Parents love their kids, but they get into trouble because the tools they have often focus on behavior and not emotional wholeness. If you're like many parents, you've tried lots of strategies to get your child to consistently act the way you think he should.

But today's children are not the same as yesterday's children. This explains why the old ways of doing things (often the way you were raised) and the old structures are not working.

You may think it is normal for children to have tantrums and be upset when they don't get their way. What I see is what most people consider "normal" isn't. Most children act similarly because parents tend to raise them the same way, but this doesn't mean children are emotionally healthy. Emotionally healthy children stand out from the crowd as being happier and more confident, focused, and compassionate.

Because today's children require a new style of parenting, you need to know how to allow freedom and self-expression while clearly setting limits that empower your child and not limit him. You need to be the best person you can be in order to be the best parent you can be.

Coaching is helpful when you have a crisis situation that has you feeling completely overwhelmed. It helps with the immediate situation and gets you started toward a deeper level of understanding when you later take the Parenting with Joy Training. Coaching is also useful when you want to focus exclusively on your unique situation or if you learn best by one-on-one interaction and support. To schedule an appointment, call 650-960-6895.

Schedule an Inspiring, Practical Talk or Workshop for Your Group

We assist parents to discover and develop their natural ability to relate easily and joyfully with their child. All of our workshops are designed to give parents the key insights and understandings they need to be the loving, joyous parent they desire to be. Parents make profound changes in their behavior when they know these essential principles to parenting success.

We use self-reflection, experiential exercises, and discussion to deepen the learning each parent receives. These tools help parents access their own inner guidance and knowledge. Then they are able to see effective ways to improve their own choices and actions, which in turn allows their child to improve her behavior also.

Empower parents and staff to have more joy and ease with children. Learn about the wide selection of workshop topics we offer by going to the following web page: http://joywithchildren.com.

Recommended Resources

1. *The Continuum Concept: In Search of Happiness Lost*, Jean Liedloff, Da Capo Press, 1986.

2. *Free at Last: The Sudbury Valley School*, Daniel Greenberg, Sudbury Valley School Press, 1995.

3. *Last Child in the Woods: Saving Our Children from Nature-Deficit Disorder*, Richard Louv, Algonquin Books, 2008.

4. *How Children Learn*, John Holt, Da Capo Press, 1995.

5. *How Children Fail*, John Holt, Da Capo Press, 1995.

6. *Teach Your Own: The John Holt Book of Homeschooling*, John Holt and Pat Farenga, Da Capo Press, 2003.

7. *Connection Parenting: Parenting through Connection instead of Coercion, Through Love instead of Fear,* Pam Leo, Wyatt-MacKenzie Publishing, 2002.

8. *Punished by Rewards: The Trouble with Gold Stars, Incentive Plans, A's, Praise, and Other Bribes,* Alfie Kohn, Replica Books, 2001.

9. *Everyday Blessings: The Inner Work of Mindful Parenting,* Myla Kabat-Zinn and Jon Kabat-Zinn, Hyperion, 1998.

10. Alliance for Transforming the Lives of Children (aTLC), http://atlc.org/.

11. Alternative Education Resource Organization (AERO), http://www.educationrevolution.org/.

12. ChildSpirit Institute, http://www.childspirit.org/.

About the Author

Connie has always been passionate about empowering others to find joy and trust in their relationships and to express their natural gifts freely.

Because she longed to help people find happiness and freely express their innate creative gifts, Connie studied extensively to expand her knowledge about empowering children and adults. She studied psychology at Boston University and California State University, where she earned her MA.

Her deep desire to work with children and to empower them led her to teach children of all ages in the public schools. She often worked with students who were considered "at risk", loving and accepting their uniqueness and discovering how adults either limit or empower children through their interactions with them.

In working with these "at risk" youth, she learned many important principles and had the great joy of connecting deeply with her students. She has had many experiences of being profoundly touched, respected, admired, and loved by her students, which still bring tears to her eyes. The beauty and brilliance within children inspires her.

When Connie became a mother, she made two intentions her priority—nurturing her relationship with her son and supporting him to be the person he naturally wanted to be. She explored new dimensions in parenting and deepened her understanding of a child's joyous inner spirit. She cherishes the honest, loving relationship she continues to share with her son Orion.

Today Connie shares the insights she has learned to nurture emotional wholeness in young people and to empower them to let their light shine brightly. She delights in teaching parents and educators how to

About the Author

read the manual their child and students came with
and to find the joy and ease in relating with children.

Connie Allen, M.A
Family and Education Coach

Joy With Children
Connie@JoyWithChildren.com
http://JoyWithChildren.com

Give a Gift of Joy!

This book makes a great gift or fundraiser. Give it to yourself, a friend, a mother or father-to-be, a teacher, or child care giver. Use it to raise funds for your school or favorite charity. Large quantity discounts are available upon request.

Quantity	Discount	Unit Price*
5 to 9	5%	$ 9.50
10 to 49	10%	$ 9.00
50 to 99	20%	$ 8.00
100 to 199	30%	$ 7.00
200 to 299	40%	$ 6.00
300 to 499	50%	$ 5.00
>500	60%	$ 4.00

* Shipping and handling not included.

For quantity orders, contact Metacreative Press at 866-756-8679 or email sales@metacreativepress.com.

Percentage of Profits to Benefit Global Fund for Children

THE GLOBAL FUND FOR
Children

A percentage of the pre-tax profits from every book will be donated to the Global Fund for Children. The Global Fund for Children's mission is to advance the dignity of children and youth around the world. GFC pursues its mission by making small grants to innovative community-based organizations working with some of the world's most vulnerable children and youth, complemented by a dynamic media program that, through books, documentary photography, and film, highlights the issues affecting children and celebrates the global society in which we all live.

For more information about Global Fund for Children, visit their web site at www.globalfundforchildren.org.